Beyond a Firm Handshake

21 Ways to Communicate You're the Right Person for the Job

2nd Edition

by

SARI DE LA MOTTE

Edited by Rachel Beohm

For Barbara

Table of Contents

Acknowledgements

Acknowledgements

This book would not have been written without the support and encouragement of several key people. To Stacey Lane, thank you for your continued guidance of my own career, and for lending your expertise to this book. To Corey Eubanks, this was your idea in the first place! Thank you so much for thinking of it, waiting for me to finish it, and helping get it out into the world. To my husband Kevin, thank you for putting up with my many months of writing and being unavailable, inattentive and sometimes inhuman. I love you.

This book, however, would not be here without my editor and friend, Rachel Beohm. You corrected every comma, dot or dash, but more importantly, you helped me get what was in my head down on the page. You were unbelievably patient, you encouraged me to keep going when I wanted to quit, and you stayed up late editing when we were on deadline. You believed in this book from the very beginning, and you believe in me. This book is as much yours as it is mine. Thank you.

Sari de la Motte

FORTE

2nd edition: July 2016

www.nonverbalFORTE.com

Introduction

You're qualified. So what?

"I don't get it," thought David. "I had all the qualifications they were looking for! Why didn't I get the job?"

Simply put, in an interview, **no one cares about your qualifications.**

All candidates chosen for a face-to-face interview are qualified. Hiring managers simply don't have *time* to interview unqualified candidates. If you didn't meet the necessary requirements for the position, you wouldn't be there, period. So if your qualifications won't win you the position, what will?

Kick-ass communication skills.

You only get one shot. The interview has nothing to do with how qualified you are and everything to do with how you communicate. During the first few seconds—often before uttering a word—you make an impression on the interviewer.[1] Good or bad, this impression will be hard to change. Within 20 minutes the hiring manager will decide whether or not to hire you.[2]

The interview is where the rubber meets the road—does the real flesh and blood person match what is on paper? You may be the smartest, most capable person in the world, but if you aren't able to communicate it in an interview, you're toast.

Every message includes three components. First, there's the content: *what* you say. Then, there's the delivery: *how* you say it. Third, there's the reception: did the listener receive your intended message? An effective message requires all three parts. For example, you can say the right thing, but if you deliver it poorly, no one cares. Or you can have your delivery down pat, but if you don't know what you're trying to say, it won't matter. Finally, you can have your message down and your delivery mastered, but if you aren't in tune with your listener, you miss the mark.

Nonverbal communication transmits the majority of any message.[3] *What* you say isn't as important as *how* you say it. Research shows that if there is a mismatch between verbal and nonverbal communication, the listener believes the nonverbal message <u>every single time</u>.[4] You may *think* you are getting your message across, but if you aren't mindful of your nonverbal communication you may be sending mixed messages.

But don't other interview books talk about nonverbal communication, or what they call "body language?" Sure, but it's usually a few basic paragraphs.

You'll hear suggestions like, "Use a firm handshake," "Maintain eye contact," and "Sit with good posture."

To which most job seekers respond, "Well, duh."

---

[1] Ron and Caryl Krannich. <u>You Should Hire Me! Interview Secrets to Get the Job You Love</u>. (Manassas Park, VA: Impact Publications, 2008), 73.
[2] Cynthia Shapiro, <u>What Does Somebody Have to Do to Get a Job Around Here? 44 Insider Secrets That Will Get You Hired</u> (New York: St. Martin's Griffin, 2008), 134.
[3] Albert Mehrabian and Morton Wiener, "Decoding of Inconsistent Communications," *Journal of Personality and Social Psychology* (1967): **6** (1): 109–114.
[4] Ibid. 109-114.

This book is different. Instead of offering obvious advice, *Beyond a Firm Handshake* provides you with 21 concrete and practical ways to communicate you're the right person for the job. We'll discuss all three components of your message, but spend most of our time looking at the nonverbal elements of delivery and reception.

The media often portrays nonverbal communication as a way to control situations or people. But to be clear, this book *isn't* about using nonverbal techniques to coerce people into giving you a job (something that is impossible anyway). The intent is to learn how to communicate as clearly as possible—not to manipulate, deceive or "put on a show." If you don't believe in yourself, or have the necessary skills, body language tips won't get you the job. Nonverbal communication skills cannot substitute for real, authentic communication.

—◆—

However, how you communicate nonverbally can make or break the interview. Good nonverbal communication skills won't guarantee you'll get what you want, but sending the wrong nonverbal message could ensure that you *don't*. Excellent communication skills will always help you; poor skills will weaken your attempts.

I know this because I've worked with thousands of individuals over the past fifteen years as a communications consultant. I've helped people prepare sales presentations, go for promotions, deal with difficult co-workers and yes, prepare for interviews. I've been featured in newspaper articles, magazine interviews and on television, and my message has never wavered: If you want to become a successful communicator, you must increase your nonverbal intelligence.

Beyond a Firm Handshake: 21 Ways to Communicate You're the Right Person for the Job goes beyond a firm handshake and other obvious "body language" advice—although I've included some for fun—and gives you practical tools to help you increase your nonverbal intelligence. This will ensure you communicate clearly, leading to increased interviewing capacity, and eventually, the job of your dreams.

If you're looking for a job, going for a promotion or just brushing up on your interview skills, I invite you read along and discover the surprising power of nonverbal communication.

1

Communicate Persuasively

You only have three seconds.

"This job is perfect for me!" thought Martha, digging up her resume. She couldn't wait to get out of advertising since earning her degree in graphic design. "Too bad the position closes so soon, or I'd brush up this old resume." She looked it over hurriedly. "Oh well," she said to herself, "I'll just add my degree and nail the interview."

But she never received a call from the hiring manager.

Jacob spent hours on his resume. He included all of his work experience, schooling and references. He added extra-curricular activities to show he was a well-rounded person. He never got called for an interview, so he continued to tinker with his resume, thinking perhaps he'd missed something important.

His resume had grown to three pages.

Both Martha and Jacob made important resume mistakes. Martha failed to tailor her resume to her audience. Jacob assumed the hiring manager would read his long resume. Neither Jacob nor Martha knew how to communicate persuasively.

Hiring managers simply don't have *time* to look over every single resume they receive. They give it a glance, get a gut feeling about it, and move it to either the "yes" pile or the "no" pile. It is estimated that less than 1% of resumes ever result in a call for an interview.[5] Your resume must persuade the hiring manager to read it in three seconds or less.[6] Since you aren't there in person, it must do this nonverbally.

Get rid of the notion that the resume is an informational document listing your qualifications, work history and education. Getting called for an interview has little to do with what your resume contains, and everything to do with what your resume nonverbally communicates. In fact, in terms of securing an interview, your resume is *the* most important nonverbal, because **nothing happens until and unless your resume persuades someone to read it.**

So how can you ensure your resume communicates persuasively?

Be Concise.

Resume writers often worry about leaving out something important. But understand this: **Long resumes don't get read.**[7] Period. Hiring managers often get hundreds of resumes in one day. If you think someone is poring over your resume, considering each job title and responsibility you've had, think again.

Many job seekers think their resume should include everything. Big mistake. **The resume's main job is to entice the hiring manager to find out**

---

[5] Shapiro 6.
[6] Ibid. 8.
[7] There are some exceptions, of course. CV's can be longer and are standard in educational fields, for example.

more about you. Your resume is an advertisement. Attention-grabbing advertisements don't list every feature of the product being sold, just the "top" qualities that invite the customer to learn more. Provide enough information to engage interest and prove you are a worthy candidate. Giving too much information overwhelms the hiring manager—the last thing you want or need.

A long resume sends the message that you lack confidence and feel the need to over-explain. Effective "advertisements" let the product speak for itself. A short, concise resume is respectful and confident. It nonverbally communicates, "I know you are inundated with prospects. Here is a summary of why you should find out more about me."

Keep it Simple.

The most successful resumes are simple; key qualifications and information are easy to find. Use traditional fonts, have paragraphs of uniform sizes, and forgo lots of boldface or underlining. Keep the look clean by avoiding too much text, so that your qualifications stand out.

You might be tempted to get attention through gimmicks. Don't! Colored paper, polka-dotted paper, perfumed resumes or resumes printed on paper that isn't 8 ½" by 11" are huge no-nos. From a nonverbal perspective, they'll get you attention, but not the kind you want. Hiring managers look for confidence, and a candidate that resorts to gimmicky strategies just screams, "Trying too hard!" Let your resume stand on its own.

Finally, **don't try to impress by listing skills you don't have.** Companies are willing to train if they like the candidate. Never lie about qualifications, education or experience.

Target the Organization.

If I'm not in the market for a new vacuum cleaner, vacuum cleaner ads, no matter how attractive, won't catch my attention. Likewise, your resume must target the organization. Craft a resume that accurately captures your uniqueness and yet visually represents that you're a good fit. For example, pay attention to style in visual arts fields, or technical language for engineering and science jobs. Your resume may change depending on the company. Carefully match the look and feel of your resume to the organization.

In addition, leave out information that makes you appear overqualified. List accurate job information, emphasizing the qualifications that make you a good fit for <u>this</u> position. Listing irrelevant skills and experience in the hopes of impressing the hiring manager will send your resume directly into the "no" pile.

Your resume introduces you to the company you hope to work for. To persuade the hiring manager to call, pay attention to what it communicates nonverbally.

—◆—

This should be obvious, but ... spelling and grammar should be absolutely perfect.

2

Communicate Calmly

Surprise!

At 5:30 p.m. the phone rang. Donna was just emptying a box of spaghetti into a pot of boiling water when she picked up the phone. It was the hiring manager from a company she had applied to recently. As she shooed out her 2-year-old and turned off the stove, her pulse began to race and she started to sweat. Why on earth would the hiring manager be calling at this time of day?

Hiring managers hope to weed out unsuitable applicants over the phone to avoid wasting time with face-to-face interviews. They often design the initial phone call to surprise you. But why?

When surprised, we tend to hold our breath—or take short, shallow breaths. Shallow breathing reduces the flow of oxygen to the brain, inhibiting

9

our ability to think clearly. Believe it or not, this is exactly what the hiring manager hopes will happen.

Hiring managers know that interviewees bring their best behavior to a scheduled interview. In hopes of observing the "real you" they plan situations to catch you off guard. Companies cannot afford to make expensive recruiting mistakes, and hope to avoid hiring candidates that interview well only to find they perform poorly on the job.

To ensure you receive an invitation for a face-to-face interview, you must remain calm and composed. Do this by regulating your breathing.

Deep breathing relaxes your body and provides oxygen to the brain, so you can think rationally. In addition, how you breathe affects the people around you. We unintentionally adopt the breathing pattern of the person who is speaking.[8] Calm, focused breathing will put you *and* the hiring manager at ease.

Follow these steps beforehand to prepare for the phone screen:

Develop awareness. To sense what deep breathing feels like, begin by lying on the ground with your hands on your abdomen. Inhale slowly, and feel your abdomen rise as your lungs fill with air. Let your breath out gradually. Repeat several times. Eventually, graduate to a standing position.

Practice. Incorporate deep breathing into your everyday life—while sitting in traffic, exercising or when waiting for your kids in the school parking lot. Practice low, abdominal breathing in stressful situations and notice how it affects the tone of your voice, your state of mind and those around you. Become accustomed to the physiological sensations of calmness so you can control your breathing when nervous.

Prepare in advance. Plan ahead to minimize distractions when the phone rings. This might include a sign on the door asking visitors not to ring the bell,

---

[8] E Peper and V. Tibbetts. "Effects of Paced Breathing on Inhalation Volumes," *Proceedings of the Twenty-first Annual Meeting of the Association for Applied Psychophysiology and Biofeedback* (Wheat Ridge, CO: AAPB, 1990): 157-59.

call-waiting turned off, or a quickly accessible quiet room prepared with your resume, a pen and a pad ready for note-taking. If you are called in the car or on the bus, ask if you can call back. Once you receive the call, whether scheduled or unexpected, take a deep breath and give your full attention to the conversation.

During the phone interview:

Stand. Do not sit while being interviewed over the telephone. Standing allows you to control your breathing more easily, adds credibility to your voice and helps you remain attentive.

Rest one hand on your abdomen. This will remind you to stay aware of your breathing and allow you to monitor it more easily.

Pause before answering questions. You can't possibly breathe if you're talking nonstop. Listen to the question posed, while focusing on your breathing. When the person stops speaking, pause before answering. Pause frequently as you speak. This forces you to breathe, making you appear more confident and poised.

Not all hiring managers will attempt to surprise you, but it pays to be prepared. If the hiring manager calls at an inconvenient time, ask if you can call back—this is totally acceptable. However, it may not always be possible. In these cases, focused breathing will assist you in communicating calmly regardless of the circumstances.

—◆—

This should be obvious, but ... if given the chance to choose the time of your phone interview, never, ever schedule it while commuting, bathing

(I've heard of this happening) or doing any other activity that won't allow you to fully concentrate.

3

Communicate Carefully

Treat or ... trick?

After applying for several positions in pharmaceutical sales, Sandra received a phone call. When the hiring manager identified herself, Sandra's pulse quickened. This company was her first choice, and she knew competition was stiff. Yet right away she sensed this interview would go well. The hiring manager was so friendly; it felt like talking to a close friend. Within a matter of minutes she relaxed, answering the hiring manager's questions with ease. "I can't believe how well this is going," she thought to herself. They talked for almost half an hour, even swapping stories about their autistic sons. When Sandra hung up, her confidence was through the roof. The hiring manager obviously liked her and said to expect a call soon.

But the company never contacted her again.

What Sandra thought was a treat was actually a trick. The hiring manager could not legally ask Sandra about her personal life, yet the friendly tone of the call fooled her. Instead of communicating carefully, Sandra willingly shared private information. That left her with no recourse once the company deemed her a risk due to her son's health issues.

Just like hiring managers hope to see the "real you" by surprising you, they also hope you'll betray possible liabilities in your personal life. They may reject candidates with small children, health issues or smokers. You may be too old or too young, too ethnic or too religious, or in some cases, not religious enough.

Hiring managers will attempt to disarm you by being "friendly" and offering up personal stories. Because we want to create rapport, we often respond in kind. This is exactly what the hiring manager hopes will happen. The friendliness is often a ruse to trick you into divulging personal information they can't legally ask.

Many job seekers think that because employers cannot legally discriminate, it's okay to offer up personal information. Wrong, wrong, wrong. Although the law prevents discrimination in hiring, you put yourself at risk by doing so. Discriminatory hiring practices are notoriously difficult to prove—especially within the context of a verbal exchange. Don't assume the law protects you. **Protect yourself by communicating carefully.**

We can communicate carefully *and* establish rapport by connecting with our interviewer nonverbally. Since nonverbal communication transmits the majority of the message, *how* we speak makes a bigger impact than *what* we say. Respectfully accommodating your interviewer's communication style silently communicates understanding, which builds rapport.

For example, every morning, my husband and I get up at 6 a.m. and walk to the gym. And <u>every</u> <u>single</u> <u>morning</u> the receptionist greets us with an overly-cheery, high-pitched, "Morning, guys!!"

That early in the morning, such perkiness makes me want to rip her face off.

It's not that she doesn't mean well; she obviously does. But her exuberance does *not* communicate understanding. One glance at my facial expression would tell any nonverbally intelligent person I need a more sedate greeting at six in the morning.

So how does this work on the phone? On the phone, we can't read facial expressions, but we can hear voice tone. During the phone interview, you can accommodate the interviewer by modulating your voice.

The next time you're at a coffee shop or other public place, listen to the sound of the voices around you. You'll discover a vast range of voice patterns. Some people speak quickly, their words tumbling hurriedly out of their mouths; others speak slowly and deliberately. Some speak with short, clipped words and sentences; others use long phrases and multi-syllabic words that ramble on for what seems an interminable amount of time, rather like this sentence.

You'll also notice differences in tone. Some people will speak with a flat voice that curls down at the ends of sentences. Think, for example, of Sean Connery saying, "Bond. James Bond." Others have a lilt to their voices and often curl upwards at the ends of statements. Recall the warm, inviting voice of Mr. Rogers: "Won't you be my neighbor?"

Consider famous people and try identifying their voice patterns. Morgan Freeman? More at the James Bond end of the spectrum. Goldie Hawn? Closer to the Mr. Rogers end of the spectrum. To practice, you can also identify voice patterns of people you know in real life.

Listen carefully to how the hiring manager speaks. If you hear the James Bond voice pattern, respond by curling your voice down. You can practice by tipping your chin down at the ends of statements. If the hiring manager speaks with a voice that is rhythmic and curls up, curl your voice up also. Practice by slightly bobbing your head up and down as you talk. If the hiring manager speaks quickly or with short sentences, keep your answers short and sweet, too.

Matching the style of the hiring manager communicates: "We speak the same language."

Always remember that the hiring manager's loyalty rests with the company, not with you. To communicate carefully, avoid disclosing personal information; instead, nonverbally demonstrate understanding to establish rapport.

— ♦ —

This should be obvious, but ... don't mimic the interviewer. Speak in your own voice, but match the nonverbal tone and inflection of the person you are speaking with.

4

Communicate Competently

If you think you can wing it, think again.

"What's the point of preparing ahead of time? I have no idea what questions they'll ask anyway."

In this changing job market, competition for available jobs is fiercer than ever. In the past, a face-to-face interview gave you a pretty good shot at getting the job. No longer. With sometimes hundreds of people competing for one job, you must prepare in advance so you can communicate competently in the interview.

Nonverbal communication comprises the majority of any message. But you can't focus on getting your message across *if you don't know what the message is*. You must have the verbal portion of your message down before focusing on the nonverbal presentation. How you gesture, what your voice sounds like, how you look—none of these things matter if you're stumbling over your words.

To communicate competently, prepare your message in advance.

To start, **research the company**. Find the mission statement online. Look through company literature. Talk to people familiar with the organization. What are the company's goals? What problems does the organization face? To demonstrate your compatibility in the interview, discover the needs of the company in advance.

After researching the company, look for ways to **align your strengths and accomplishments** with the needs of the organization. Begin by asking yourself questions: What makes me unique? What are my strengths? What have I accomplished? Then ask: How do these things make me a good fit for this position?

Next, **prepare examples.** Use the following formula:

Strength + Application = Outcome

For example, "I understand this position requires public speaking. I deliver presentations well. In my last job I trained new sales staff and consistently received high marks for my presentation content and style. For example, last fall I put together a workshop…" Prepare several examples so you are ready to answer questions as they come up. People love stories, so include details. Finally, **practice.** Get familiar with your content by running through it in advance. Practice verbalizing your stories and examples so you aren't searching for words or awkwardly hesitating in the interview.

Don't assume you can wing the interview. Be prepared! Nonverbal communication transmits the majority of any message, but that doesn't mean you can afford to ignore the message itself.

—◆—

This should be obvious, but … don't memorize answers. Practice your content ahead of time, but avoid sounding like a robot.

5

Communicate Professionally

It's what's on the <u>outside</u> that counts.

"White socks with black shoes? A shirt so wrinkled he must have just pulled it from the dryer? Uh… no thanks! Next candidate, please."
"His shoes were so scuffed, I couldn't take my eyes off them."
"She actually came dressed like a streetwalker. It was incredible."

The minute you walk through the door the hiring manager will make assumptions about your capabilities, intelligence and performance based on what you look like. Unfair or not, up to 80% of job applicants are rejected based on how they are dressed.[9] "Inappropriate attire" is one of the top ten complaints of hiring managers.[10]

---

[9] Krannich 73.
[10] Davis 91.

Yet, "Dress professionally" is incomplete advice. You must understand *why* dressing professionally makes such a significant impact.

Most of us dress appropriately for interviews without giving it a second thought. Yet understanding the importance of appearance will assist you in avoiding other, less-obvious mistakes. You dress suitably not to impress, but to avoid detracting from the primary focus: you. Ill-fitting, wrinkled, casual clothing draws attention to itself, when you want the focus to be on why you're the best person for the job. Communicate professionally so that the hiring manager can stay focused on YOU, not your clothing, earrings, hairstyle or accessories.

Keep these tips in mind:

Get expert advice. A consultant can go shopping with you to pick out the perfect attire and will assist you with accessories and grooming. At the very least, consult a good book on the subject. Dress the part, but in a way that minimizes distractions.

Look as though you fit in, not stick out. Professionalism in one industry may be different than another. Hiring managers want to know if you suit the company. Your clothing will answer that question before you even open your mouth. A hiring manager from a laid-back company recently shared with me the following story: During a series of interviews a man arrived wearing a suit and tie. The three interviewers were instantly turned off. "He was obviously trying too hard," he said. A few candidates later, a man walked in wearing jeans and a black T-shirt. The hiring manager told me, "We were immediately intrigued. This showed confidence. It said this guy was an individual but also knew our culture. Our CEO often wears jeans and a T-shirt. It made him seem like he fit in."

Study the industry carefully and match accordingly. When in doubt, overdress, but this is where your research really pays off.

Avoid flashy clothing and accessories. Maybe you love your red blazer, but you don't want to be known as "the lady in the red blazer who interviewed here last Tuesday." You want to be remembered for how you'll benefit the company, not by your attention-grabbing clothing.

Have you ever received an entrée in a restaurant and been afraid to eat it? You stare at the four-inch tower in the middle of the plate wondering where to start. The intricate presentation of the food usurps the entire point: What it tastes like. Likewise, dressing in a way that focuses the attention on your clothing, rather than what you offer, detracts from your primary message. Dress professionally so there are *fewer* distractions, not more.

Never wear anything you just bought. The interview is **not** the time to find out that your skirt rides too high when you cross your legs or that your shirt collar itches terribly. Looking uncomfortable in your own skin or calling attention to your undergarments will detract from your overall presentation. Wear clothing you've already road-tested, or do a few trial runs in your new clothing ahead of time.

Details matter. I once spoke with a hiring manager who didn't hire an otherwise appropriately dressed candidate because she wore a black bra under her white shirt. Pay attention to details such as underclothing, accessories, make-up and hairstyle. Professional appearance goes beyond clothing.

Skip the fragrances. Avoid wearing perfume, cologne or highly scented deodorants. Let the receptionist announce your arrival, not your perfume.

Your clothing can add to your confidence. Professional clothing does wonders for your self-image. When you look the part, you feel the part. This will translate in the interview.

—◆—

This should be obvious, but ... do wear clothes. NEVER try to get attention by showing up in a bunny suit, bikini, or god-forbid, naked. True story:

A man interviewed for the position of bartender. Midway through, he excused himself and went to the restroom. A few minutes later, he returned, but his clothes didn't come with him! He got attention, but he didn't get the job. You want the hiring manager to focus on your credibility and compatibility, not on your wrinkled skirt, scuffed shoes, or, ahem, bare bottom.

6

Communicate Selectively

Do sweat the small stuff.

Travelling to my sister's for Thanksgiving, I took Interstate 5 from Portland down to Los Angeles. Near the Grapevine, I entered a tunnel. When I emerged, I spied a police car on the side of the road. Afraid of getting a ticket, I slammed on my brakes, as did every other car that came through the tunnel. But there was no threat. The police car was empty.

A police car sends a powerful nonverbal message whether it contains a police officer or not. Objects are nonverbal and can add or detract from our presentation. Malcolm Gladwell, in his groundbreaking book *Blink: The Power of Thinking Without Thinking* shares a research study that illustrates this point. Study participants visited the dorm rooms of students they did not know. They took notes on what they learned about the students by simply viewing their possessions. Researchers were astonished to find that in several key areas, the strangers more accurately described the students than close friends.[11]

Our "stuff" says a lot about us. In an interview, pay attention to what you bring since it can powerfully affect the impression you make.

Watch out for the following:

Purses. A purse nonverbally screams "personal life" when we want to put our most credible, business persona forward. Bring a briefcase or laptop bag instead.

Phones. Attention is a precious resource these days as everyone is glued to the screens of their smartphones. AVOID THIS. If you must bring your phone with you, turn it off and don't bring it out unless necessary (i.e., to check your schedule and make a follow-up interview appointment). If you'd like to take notes on your phone, tell the interviewer you are taking notes and NOT sending messages. If the temptation to check your notifications is too great, stick to good old pen and paper.

Don't even look at your phone in the reception area. Scrolling through your phone while waiting sends the message that you aren't fully engaged. It can ruin your chances before you even get into the interview room.

Keys. Keys make noise and can create an awkward-looking bump in pockets. Take your car key off the key chain and slip it into your pocket or briefcase. Leave the rest of your keys in the glove compartment.

Food and Beverages. Never bring food or beverages to an interview. Don't bring a travel mug or stop at Starbucks on the way. Doing so communicates that you don't take the interview seriously. Likewise, avoid bringing coffee for the hiring manager. One job seeker did this—hoping to make a good impression—and managed to spill coffee all over the hiring manager's desk.

---

[11] Malcolm Gladwell. Blink: The Power of Thinking Without Thinking. (New York: Back Bay Books, 2007), 34 – 37.

Coat. You can wear a coat to the interview, but once you arrive, take it off and hang it in the lobby. Wearing a coat communicates you're only staying a short while: not the impression you want to make.

Other Personal Items. This includes shopping bags, umbrellas, sunglasses, books, etc. Leave these items in the car, or in the case of an umbrella, the lobby.

What you **should** bring to an interview:

Briefcase or Laptop Bag. Your briefcase should be in good condition without scratches or scuffs. Clean and organize the interior, removing extraneous paperwork or unopened mail.

Pen or Pencil. Bring something to make notes and fill out additional paperwork. Make sure the pen works and the pencil is sharpened.

Resume. You probably won't need it, but on the off chance you do, be prepared.

A List of Questions. Hopefully, you've done your homework about the organization. If so, prepare a list of questions to demonstrate your interest in the company.

Just as we instinctively react when we see a police car, hiring managers experience gut-level reactions to the objects we bring to the interview. Communicate selectively by preparing your interview image carefully.

—◆—

This should be obvious, but ... don't bring other *people* to the interview. One man brought his mother, who knocked on the door in the middle of the interview to ask how much longer she had to wait.

7

Communicate Consistently

Your interview begins in the parking lot.

As Angela rushed to her interview, she checked the mirror to make sure she had applied her make-up correctly. Her husband had woken up with a cold, leaving her to take the kids to school, and she was running ten minutes behind. As she pulled into the parking lot she chucked her cigarette out of the window and popped a breath mint. Once parked, she exited the car, smoothed out her skirt and put on her earrings. Looking in the side-view mirror, she picked at a poppy seed stuck between her teeth from breakfast. Rattled at her late start, she entered the elevator, and didn't hear the gentleman near the front ask what floor she needed until he repeated it twice. "Floor fourteen, I think," she said, as she rummaged through her purse for the directions. As she rode the elevator up she thought, "I need to pull it together before my interview starts."

Angela failed to grasp that her interview began the minute she drove onto the premises.

Most job seekers think the interview starts once they sit in front of the hiring manager. That's a mistake. How you behave the minute you drive into the parking lot can affect the outcome of your interview.

You never know who could be watching your behavior. The person you frowned at in the parking lot could be the CEO on her way out to lunch. The man in the elevator watching you yawn and pick at your nails might be the hiring manager's friend. Your irritation over a late start to your interview may be noted by the receptionist and later passed on.

Keep in mind that anyone you come in contact with could influence whether or not you are hired. The entire time you remain on the premises—driving into the parking lot, walking to the building, riding up an elevator, sitting in the waiting area—practice a cheerful and gracious demeanor. Smile. Greet others. Be polite. You will make a positive impression and boost your confidence. At all times, avoid nervous behaviors such as smoothing your hair, fiddling with jewelry, or tugging at your clothing. You are always on display.

During my research for this book I read a story of a job seeker who ignored this rule and paid the price. Unbeknownst to him, the person conducting his interview wore a uniform from the warehouse that day and was seated at the reception desk. When the job seeker arrived, the "receptionist" asked him to fill out an application. He refused, saying he wasn't there for "that type of a job." The person behind the desk told him it was standard procedure. The job seeker replied, "Obviously, you don't understand. Get me someone with real authority." The
man behind the desk stood, introduced himself and explained that there would be no need for an interview after all.[12]

---

[12] Davis 76.

Communicate consistently from the moment you arrive. Observe this rule on your way *back* to the car as well. Don't call a friend and comment on how the interview went. If the interview begins in the parking lot, it ends there too.

— ◆ —

This should be obvious, but ... don't smoke, litter, spit or talk on your cell phone in the parking lot, elevator, lobby, or waiting area. And for goodness sake: *don't be late*. Sheesh.

8

Communicate Perceptively

Please take a seat ... and a good look around.

You arrive a little early, greet the receptionist and take a seat. Don't just wait for your interview to start. Use this prime opportunity to further your research about the company.

How? By observing company culture.

The attitudes and behaviors that characterize a specific company comprise its culture.[13] **To communicate perceptively in the interview, you must understand the company's culture.**

Hiring managers look for qualified candidates who suit the organization. Companies aren't looking for yellow pencils; but they want to know that your personality won't cause conflict or detract from business. It's one thing to be

---

[13] Michael Grinder. The Inside Track: Managing Groups. (Stout Graphics, 2008), 11-12.

able to perform the duties of the job. It's quite another to get along with your colleagues and function as a part of the team.

Companies nonverbally betray culture just like people do. While you're waiting, look for nonverbal indicators. For example:

- How did the receptionist greet you? How do people greet each other? Do they stop to chat or do they breeze on by?

- Do people use a lot of eye contact or do they tend to look at other items like papers, reports and computer screens?

- How do people sound? Do their voices curl up at the ends of statements? Or curl down?

- What body language do you see? Do people lean forward and bob their heads when communicating, or sit straight and hold their heads still?

- What does the furniture look like? Professional, square and sparse? Or inviting, soft and comfortable?

- How do people dress? Dark colors, similar styles? Or lighter colors with wild variety?

- Is food available? Do you see candy dishes, doughnuts or other snacks?

Now take this information and use it to decide whether the culture is *relationship*-orientated or *issue*-orientated. A relationship-oriented company values morale. You'll observe more eye contact, rolling voice patterns that curl up at the ends of statements, bobbing heads, comfy furniture, food, etc. An issue-oriented company values productivity. You'll observe less eye contact, flat voice patterns that curl down at the ends of statements, more severe furniture and fewer "distractions" like candy and snacks.

Once you identify company culture, highlight your most relevant skills in the interview. For an issue-oriented company, communicate your ability to get projects done in an efficient and timely manner. For a relationship-oriented company, convey your ability to get along with others and work as a team. You can, of course, do both. But you need to demonstrate that you fit the culture.

Become a keen observer as soon as you walk in, so you can communicate perceptively when sitting across from the hiring manager.

—◆—

This should be obvious, but ... don't be, uh, obvious. Take a look around while you wait, but avoid staring. Staring at people is creepy.

9

Communicate Purposefully

A firm handshake is just the beginning.

It's time.

The hiring manager greets you. You stand and shake hands.

Whew. The first impression is over. Or is it?

Not by a long shot. What you do in the next ten minutes will solidify your impression in the mind of the hiring manager. You must communicate purposefully and go beyond a firm handshake.

We often focus so intently on what we plan on *saying* that we ignore what we're *doing*. For example, you might walk into the hiring manager's office and take the first seat you see, when he planned to ask you to sit elsewhere. Already you've inadvertently communicated an inability to follow directions. Think these things don't matter? Think again.

Your primary purpose in an interview is to communicate that you are the best person for the job. To do this, you need to control how you come across. If you make a negative first impression, you can't fix it later. You must communicate purposefully from the moment you meet the interviewer. Don't leave your first impression up to chance.

Communicate on purpose by managing the following nonverbal behaviors:

Follow the hiring manager's lead concerning seating. Never take a seat before being offered one; wait until you've been directed to a chair to sit down. If the hiring manager doesn't offer you a seat, ask before taking one.

Don't touch anything. The interviewer's office is his personal space. Never pick up or touch anything that isn't yours.

Take a breath. After taking a seat, breathe deeply. Telling yourself to "remain calm" doesn't help, but breathing well will calm you down and affect everything else you do in the interview.

Smile. When nervous, some people tense their faces, resulting in what appears to be a scowl. (I recently found I do this!) After taking a breath, make sure your face is relaxed. Smile as you wait for the interview to begin.

Let the hiring manager begin. Never launch into the interview by speaking first. Take your cues from the hiring manager.

Be careful about where you place your hands. Avoid crossing your arms or grasping them in front of your crotch. Instead, hold arms parallel to the ground by resting them on the armrest, or, if no armrests are available, placing them on your lap with fingertips lightly touching. This conveys that you have high expectations of yourself and the interview.

Don't fidget. I always suggest role-playing an interview with a friend and videotaping it since most people don't have a clue about what they do when under stress or pressure. You might find that you play with your earrings or tug on your tie. Some women twirl their hair or sweep their bangs to one side. You might click a pen nervously or shake your foot back and forth. All of these things are distracting to the interviewer and pull the focus off of your presentation. Avoid them.

Maintain eye contact. Don't look down or dart your eyes nervously around the room. Look at your interviewer with a steady but relaxed gaze. No one can maintain eye contact the entire time, nor should they (creepy!), but make sure you're looking at the hiring manager at least 80% of the time.

First impressions matter. Your unconscious mannerisms may sabotage your image. Purposefully choose your actions to make a positive, professional impression.

—◆—

This should be obvious, but ... make sure your handshake is firm (but not *too* firm). I'm amazed that I need to mention this at all, but I STILL encounter people with a limp-fish or bone-crushing handshake.

You *won't* be able to go "beyond a firm handshake" if you don't, um, have one.

10

Communicate Attentively

The interview is a dialogue, not a monologue.

"So, tell me about yourself."

Upon hearing these words job seekers launch into their carefully prepared "speeches," thinking the interview consists only of being asked—and subsequently answering—questions.

Communication doesn't take place in a vacuum; the interview is a dialogue, not a monologue. We often think of communication as *imparting* information when in reality it consists of *exchanging* information. Good communication involves a give and take. Focus only on your communication and you will miss out on inside information essential to successfully presenting yourself as the ideal candidate.

In addition, listening will establish rapport. Creating a personal connection with your interviewer can make a big difference. We all want to feel heard and understood, whether we're speaking to our supervisors, spouses, friends or potential new employees. Listening conveys that you want to hear the interviewer's point of view. When you listen attentively, you make a positive impression and appear more likeable—a huge advantage to any job seeker.

As a society, we don't listen well. Go to any social event and you'll find plenty of people who are willing to talk about themselves, but few skilled in the art of listening. In school, we spend most of our time learning to read and write, less time learning to speak and no time learning to listen. In an interview, the person who listens well will outshine the other candidates.

Keep this in mind when attempting to communicate attentively: It's one thing to listen, but quite another to *communicate* that you're listening. You must do both. Listen, but also nonverbally convey that you are engaged and alert.

Communicate attentively by:

Listening with your body. Face your interviewer. Make steady eye contact; avoid looking over the interviewer's shoulder, around the room, down at the floor or at your lap. Lean forward, nod your head or tilt it to the side. Make sounds like "mmhmm" and "ah," or use phrases like "yes," "I see" or "I understand."

Waiting to speak. Give the interviewer time to finish speaking before jumping in. Avoid tapping your foot, drumming your fingers or opening and closing your mouth while the interviewer speaks, indicating your boredom or impatience as you "wait your turn." Concentrate on what the hiring manager says instead of formulating what you plan to say in response.

Allowing silence. Don't jump in the second the interviewer pauses. Allow for breaks in the conversation; wait a moment after the interviewer stops before speaking.

Asking clarifying questions. Ask questions that indicate your interest and encourage the interviewer to continue speaking. For example, after hearing that the previous employee was fired for not working well with others you might say, "It sounds like you highly value teamwork. Can you tell me more about your expectations in this area?"

You must listen, and communicate you have listened, for the speaker to feel heard. If you do all the talking, you won't create a connection with your interviewer or learn anything valuable.

Remember that communication is a two-way street; engage in a dialogue to communicate attentively.

—◆—

This should be obvious, but ... don't ask so many questions that you never answer any yourself. You need to listen *and* talk.

11

Communicate Insightfully

Forget the job description.

Administrative assistant needed to assist professional consultant with day-to-day activities of running a business. Flexible schedule, 1 – 3 mornings a week, 3 – 4 hours a day. Ideal position for college communication majors, retired/part-time educators, or former business professionals.

Applicants will be subject to a background search. Send resume with salary expectations.

Qualifications

- *Highly organized, punctual and professional*
- *Proficient on MS Office (Word and Excel skills needed) and Entourage*
- *Excellent typing skills*

- *Ability to work independently but willing to take direction*

- *Superior written and verbal communication skills*

- *A sharp focus on detail and accuracy*

- *Ability to prioritize competing tasks*

- *An interest in education/business communication*

I ran this ad on Craigslist in an attempt to hire my first administrative assistant. I narrowed the number of applicants down to four: a student, a former executive turned stay-at-home-mom, a current administrative assistant who wanted more work, and a former high school teacher and published poet.

I scheduled the interviews back-to-back on a weekday afternoon at a coffee shop. Each candidate was qualified, albeit some more than others. I was leaning toward the third candidate, as her qualifications and experience matched my ad almost perfectly.

And then I met Val.

I liked her immediately. She was funny and disarming. She spoke openly about her lack of experience, joking that being an administrative assistant couldn't be more difficult than managing a classroom of teenagers. I asked her the same questions I had asked the other candidates, but soon we moved off-topic. We discussed how I got into the business, how isolating my day-to-day work was, and before I knew it, we had moved from the coffee shop to the bar across the street. What had originally been scheduled as a 45-minute interview stretched into a 3-hour get-to-know-you session. I drove home and tried to talk myself into the more "qualified" candidate. But in my heart I knew I wanted Val. I called her the next morning and offered her the job.

I tell this story frequently because Val communicated insightfully. I *thought* I wanted an administrative assistant, but I really wanted companionship. I was looking for someone to partner with. Val spoke to this need and I hired her.

Forget the job description. A want ad can't begin to capture the company's true needs and wants. The hiring manager will divulge this information during the interview if you know what to listen for.

When my husband, Kevin, first starting working as a chef, he secured an interview with an upscale market. This store attracts chefs from all over the city because of "lifestyle" scheduling, high hourly wages and medical benefits. It isn't unusual to wait a year and a half for a position with this company to open up.

The ad stated the company needed a line-cook with knowledge of natural and organic foods. But in the interview the head chef said things like, "The lunch rush here is crazy" or "We all help each other out whenever we can" or "Although the atmosphere here is more relaxed than most restaurants it still can get hectic." Kevin had never worked as a line cook and knew little about organic food; but he knew that cooks who couldn't manage pressure didn't last long in the kitchen. Kevin's previous experience as a camera assistant in Hollywood handling expensive film taught him how to deal with stressful situations and tight deadlines. He highlighted this experience in the interview, drawing parallels between camera assisting and restaurant work. He got the job.

Listen carefully to the words and phrases your interviewer uses. In my interview with Val, I said things like, "I've had to do everything myself" or "Working alone has been tough" or "It's difficult when you don't have anyone to run ideas by." Val picked up on these clues and communicated her ability to collaborate with me instead of focusing on what I stated in the ad. Likewise, by listening carefully, Kevin knew that experience with organic foods mattered less than an ability to function in a demanding environment.

Word choice is nonverbal. We communicate our true message, in part, through the phrases we use. The savvy job seeker will hear what isn't being said by "reading between the lines." I never said, "I need a companion," and Kevin's interviewer never said, "We need someone who can deal with stress." By picking up on the theme of the words, both Val and Kevin identified the real issues and addressed them.

The moral of the story is this: If you lack experience or qualifications, communicate insightfully and the company will train you. Listen carefully and read between the lines. Don't get stuck on job descriptions.

—◆—

This should be obvious, but ... don't be arrogant. Highlight relevant skills while remaining open to learning new ones.

12

Communicate Compatibly

What it really means to be "likeable."

In an interview, you must communicate a variety of things—your qualifications, your compatibility with the organization and your professionalism, for starters. But all things being equal, you'll ultimately be offered the job because the employer *likes* you more than the other candidates.

But what does it mean to be "likeable"?

One theory claims that interviewers "like" candidates that are similar to them. Armed with this information, job seekers think they should "mirror" the interviewer, in hopes of establishing rapport. They copy body language, leaning forward or back, crossing or uncrossing their legs, in order to match the hiring manager. Mirroring body language is like wearing the same outfit as your interviewer: you appear similar on the outside, but it doesn't provide any sort of connection. It feels silly and looks even sillier, and can come off as manipulative.

I'm going to suggest that the most "likeable" candidates are those who can communicate in the preferred style of the hiring manager. Good communication happens when people are in sync. Uncomfortable, tense communication leads to misunderstandings of both the content of the message, and the intent of the messenger. When we accurately assess and match the communication style of our interviewer, our "likeability quotient" increases dramatically.

If you observe carefully, you'll notice that the hiring manager will lean toward one of two communication styles: relational or positional. A hiring manager with a more relational style will seem friendly and engaging from the start, whereas the hiring manager with a more positional style will seem "all business."

A hiring manager will betray his or her communication style nonverbally. A relational hiring manager will tend to use approachable nonverbals, such as a relaxed, more open posture, whereas a positional hiring manager will tend to use authoritative nonverbals that convey credibility and expertise.

It may be helpful to think of ridiculous extremes. Extreme approachable nonverbals conjures up the image of a "Valley Girl": palms open with wrists bent, saying, "Like, gag me with a spoon, ya know?" But on the extreme end of authoritative nonverbals stands a drill sergeant with rigid posture and a short, clipped manner, yelling, "You can't handle the truth!" In an interview, you (hopefully!) won't meet extremes; the hiring manager will likely fall somewhere towards the middle but over to one side.

Hiring managers who use authoritative communication distribute weight evenly over both feet which gives them straight posture. When gesturing, their palms face down. Their voices sound flat and curl down at the ends of statements. Eye contact is limited. Hiring managers who use approachable communication stand with weight unevenly distributed. If seated, they lean forward, backward, or to the side. When gesturing, their palms face up. Their voices sound rhythmic and curl up at the ends of statements. They make more eye contact. Though neither style is better or worse than the other, both tell you something important about the interviewer.

Authoritative communication sends the message that the issue takes precedence over the relationship between parties. In other words, positional communicators wish to discuss the matter at hand rather than "wasting" time with small talk or other "personal" types of communication. The higher the level of authority, the more positional communication you will likely encounter.

Approachable communication conveys that the speaker welcomes input and values the relationship between parties. Relational communicators want to learn about you and share about themselves. You'll find more relational communication in the lower levels of an organization.

With a more positional hiring manager, the interview will likely start with the issue. With a flat, curled down voice pattern he might say, "I notice you've been out of work for six months. How do you explain this?" On the other hand, the relational hiring manager might begin by asking if you had trouble finding the office, remarking on the weather or engaging in other small talk. Interview questions will be posed in a more open-ended style with rolling voice pattern and may begin with, "Tell me about yourself."

Successful interviewing requires adapting to the style of the hiring manager.

For example, when my husband, Kevin, interviewed for a promotion, he sat down with the assistant store manager, a relational interviewer. The interview was going well until he asked Kevin to talk about how he planned to manage employees of the kitchen. As Kevin spoke about the importance of holding people accountable and changes he would like to make, he noticed his interviewer's posture shift. Previously at ease, the assistant manager now stiffened, sat upright and his voice sounded stressed. Kevin realized he had been too positional. He immediately told a story about a time he dealt with conflict, highlighting the fact that he was able to preserve the relationship and how it ended well. His interviewer relaxed and the interview got back on track.

Communicate compatibly by matching communication styles: use authoritative nonverbals with a positional interviewer, and approachable nonverbals with a relational interviewer. Mismatching with either interviewer will deem you "unlikeable."

We all feel more comfortable communicating one way or the other. Yet we must learn to communicate in a variety of ways. An interviewer is ten times more likely to hire someone who he or she feels comfortable with.[14] Effective communicators identify what type of communication will best accommodate the situation and modify their style accordingly. By doing so, we are viewed as "likeable" because communication becomes easy and free.

—◆—

This should be obvious, but ... most people use *both* authoritative and approachable communication though they may gravitate towards one end of the spectrum. Avoid labeling the hiring manager as one style or another; instead, as Kevin did, adapt your approach based on what's happening in the moment.

[14] Shapiro 109.

13

Communicate Congruently

Good on paper, great in person.

For six years I searched for a diagnosis for my inexplicable back pain. I'd had x-rays and exams, been to chiropractors and acupuncturists, but the pain stubbornly refused to go away, and none of these professionals could identify the cause. I decided to try physical therapy and made an appointment with a recommended therapist. After describing my symptoms, she immediately diagnosed the problem. I was thrilled. But things quickly went downhill. As she described the treatment options she giggled every time she paused.

"So, what I would suggest," (giggle) "is that you sign up for the yoga class I teach" (giggle) "to strengthen your lower back." (giggle) "We can also do some bio-feedback." (giggle)

I tried to ignore it. I told myself it didn't matter. But with every giggle, my confidence in her expertise decreased. Forty-three giggles later, I decided not to make a return appointment.

The number one fear of a hiring manager is hiring the wrong person. In an interview, the hiring manager must decide whether or not to take a risk on you. Since she cannot actually observe you perform the duties of the job, she must determine, based on how you communicate in the interview, how believable you are. Can you really perform the tasks needed successfully? Are you really good with people? Are you who you say you are?

You convey believability by communicating congruently, which means matching your verbal and nonverbal behavior. Remember: If there is a mismatch between verbal and nonverbal communication, the listener will believe the nonverbal message. To establish credibility, you must align what you *do* with what you *say*.

In the previous chapter we discussed using authoritative and approachable communication to match your interviewer and increase likeability. Those same nonverbal skills can be used to communicate a congruent message, with this rule of thumb:

Use authoritative voice pattern and body language when <u>sending</u> information and approachable voice pattern and body language when <u>seeking</u> information. Why? Authoritative body language implies one-way communication. It says, "I have the floor. The information I have to relate is important." Approachable communication sends the message that input is welcomed. It says, "I want to hear what you have to say. Let's dialogue. I'm interested in your thoughts."

To drive this point home, pretend that *you* are the interviewer. Let's say you're trying to find a new babysitter or pet sitter. When you ask what the potential sitter would do in the case of a fire, he answers in an approachable voice pattern, "Well? I guess if it was a little fire...? I'd probably try to put it out myself? With a fire extinguisher? But if it was a serious fire? I'd grab the kids [or pets] and my phone? And run outside? And call 9-1-1?"

How much confidence do you have in this person's ability to handle a crisis? Do you think he's a qualified sitter?

But now, let's say you've asked the same candidate if he has questions for you, and with an authoritative voice pattern he asks questions that sound much more like statements: "What are your kids [or pets] like. What happened to your previous sitter. What is the pay."

At this point, you're probably feeling a little put out and wondering who this guy thinks he is, interrogating you!

The candidate is communicating incongruently. When seeking information, use approachable voice pattern and body language to communicate interest in the answers. If he tilts his head and curls his voice up at the end of his questions, he would sound much more curious than demanding. When establishing credibility or giving information, it would be better to be authoritative. Using straight posture and a flat voice when stating how he would handle a crisis would immediately give you more assurance that he could handle the situation.

When my physical therapist asked me to describe my symptoms she used approachable voice pattern. I responded, since we tend to look longer and talk more easily with someone using approachable nonverbals. However, once it was her turn to give advice, she should have switched to authoritative nonverbals to communicate her expertise and emphasize her message. Her giggling suggested that she was unsure of her diagnosis, treatment plan, and ultimately, authority.

In an interview, your believability rests on how congruently you communicate. If you use approachable communication while discussing your qualifications, you imply that the interviewer would be wise to question your ability. Similarly, if you ask questions using authoritative communication you are less likely to get an answer.

To practice congruency, try the following: With a partner playing the hiring manager, answer a question about your qualifications. For example, the partner might say, "Tell me about your last position." As you answer, make sure you are using authoritative nonverbals by sitting up straight with weight over both feet. Turn the palms down as you gesture. End each sentence by curling the voice down. Breathe deeply and pause often.

Now, have your partner ask, "So, do you have any questions for me?" This is your cue to switch to approachable communication since you will be looking for a reply. Shift your weight to one side, turn the palms up, and end your questions by curling the voice up. Continue to breathe and pause.

Accurately sending or seeking information goes a long way in establishing your believability. **Use authoritative communication when sending information and approachable communication when seeking information.** Ensure your message gets across by communicating congruently.

—◆—

This should be obvious, but … watch out for nervous giggling, seriously. It is one sure-fire way to destroy your credibility.

14

Communicate Enthusiastically

I want to work here because ... I need a job.

Several years ago, I climbed into my car after finishing a workshop. I turned on my phone and adjusted my rearview mirror as I waited for it to power up. Suddenly, the screen lit up with several text and voice messages. Four hours earlier, my father had suffered a stroke.

I flew to his bedside where my sister, mother and I kept watch. We anxiously observed doctors and nurses filing in and out, administering medication, tests and other care. As the days began to run into each other, we became familiar with the nursing staff and could easily identify our favorites. The best nurses balanced their expertise with their concern. They skillfully performed their duties but also got to know my dad as a person. When your loved one lies helplessly in a hospital bed, you want the people taking care of him to know what they are doing. But you also want them to care.

This also applies to interviews. In an interview, it's not enough to communicate that you can *do* the job. You also have to demonstrate that you *want* the job. Organizations want qualified candidates, sure. But they also want candidates who are enthusiastic—about the position, field, company or work environment.

Awhile back, we needed a new administrative assistant at FORTE. After sifting through the resumes, I called a few potential candidates to set up interviews. After speaking with one woman on the phone, I was *sure* she was "The One." Her vibrant personality came through over the phone and her interests were right in line with what we do. I scheduled her for an interview at the end of the day, saving "the best" candidate for last.

She walked in, just as vibrant in person as she had been on the phone. She sat down at the conference table along with me and the rest of the FORTE team and I asked, "So, why do you want to work at FORTE?"

"Well," she answered, "I just need a job."

Uh, *wrong* answer.

You must communicate your enthusiasm in the interview not only for a job, but this job. How?

Speak up.

If you are passionate about the work the company does, don't hide it! Mention an article you recently read or previous experiences with the subject matter; it goes a long way in the interview. One candidate, applying for a job at a music distributor, highlighted his familiarity with the company by mentioning that several of his former clients had used their services. He used his prior knowledge to speak enthusiastically about the company and their work, and ultimately was awarded the job.

Likewise, when I hired a business manager, the candidates I most seriously considered discussed their interest in nonverbal communication and mentioned books or articles they'd read on the subject. When the decision lies between a skilled candidate, and a skilled candidate with an interest in nonverbal communication, who do you think I'm going to choose?

Communicate that you researched the company.

In the ad I ran for a business manager, I asked candidates to peruse my website and share marketing ideas. Astonishingly, many applicants ignored this request. The applicant who won the position not only followed directions, but also demonstrated an understanding of and interest in my business based on what he saw. In the interview he shared marketing ideas based on a thorough examination of my website.

There's no point in researching the company ahead of time if you don't use that information in the interview. Utilize what you've learned to ask more in-depth questions, to remark on things you found interesting and to demonstrate you've done your homework.

Use approachable body language and voice pattern when discussing your excitement for the job.

Use positional communication when discussing your expertise, work history or education. But when speaking about your enthusiasm, use approachable communication. Smile. Use more eye contact. Lean forward. Share what makes you personally excited about the position. Using approachable body language and voice pattern communicates that you want the job.

Demonstrate your interest as well as your ability. Whether we're in a hospital, courtroom, classroom or boardroom, we all want to work with people who care.

— ◆ —

This should be obvious but ... don't fake interest. If you really do just "need a job," find *something* that you can get behind. There's always something to be enthusiastic about. Find out what it is and communicate your enthusiasm for it.

15

Communicate Confidently

Act like you belong… and you will.

Leaf through a stack of interview preparation books and you'll find one theme popping up over and over again: confidence. Companies not only want qualified candidates that fit the company culture, but candidates that convey confidence.

The question is: How do you communicate confidence? Employers overlook capable applicants due to lack of confidence, and yet overly confident interviewees come off as arrogant. So what's the trick?

Here are three things you can do to communicate confidence:

First, breathe. How you breathe affects your posture, movements, and tone of voice. With shallow, nervous breathing, your posture will be stiff, your movements will be awkward and stilted, and your voice will sound edgy. When you breathe deeply, your body relaxes. Of course, you don't want to be so relaxed that you come across as bored or uninterested! Stay alert and engaged—yet, breathe well, so that your body can be still, your movements can be fluid, and your voice can be warm.

Try it: Take a small, shallow breath and hold it. Tense your muscles. Then, without relaxing or exhaling first, say, "I work well with others." How did that sound? Chances are, you sounded a bit… scary, and not at all like a positive team player. Take a few deep breaths until you feel your whole body relax. Then say the same words. Did you sound different?

Good breathing communicates comfort. By breathing well, you tell the hiring manager, "I am comfortable in this environment. I am comfortable with you." Interviewers expect candidates to be nervous, but extreme discomfort sends the signal that you don't trust your own abilities—your abilities to make it through the interview, your abilities to navigate a new position, or your abilities to perform on the job. Breathing well under pressure says, "I trust myself. I can handle this. I belong."

In addition, good breathing gets oxygen to your brain so that you can think more rationally and creatively. When you're stressed, it's easy to go into fight-or-flight. In that mode, your body reroutes oxygen from the thinking part of your brain to the instinctive part of the brain, as well as to your limbs so that you can actually fight or fly (hence nervously tapping pens or jiggling feet). But unless you're interviewing for a position at WWF, quick physical instincts probably won't help you much. Instead, breathe well so that you can answer interview questions intelligently and confidently.

Second, open up. Another way to demonstrate comfort and confidence is to keep your body language open. When we feel threatened, we either puff up outward to intimidate others or pull inward to protect ourselves (back to fight-or-flight!). Communicating confidence means showing that you *aren't* threatened. It shows, instead, that you belong. Do that by maintaining open body language.

Avoid protective body language, such as crossing your arms, sitting on your hands, or making yourself small. Also avoid "puffing up" postures, such as putting your hands on your hips, intruding into the personal space of others, or spreading your personal belongings all over as if you own the place. Just allow your body to take up as much space as it needs, without pulling in or pushing out. Prove that you're comfortable in your own skin.

Here's a sneaky tip, though: Before your interview, DO engage in some "puffing up" postures and make your body as big and expansive as possible. Put your hands on your hips or behind your head or reach right up to the sky. These large, open movements increase your testosterone, the confidence hormone. (Yes, women, you need testosterone, too!) You will not only *look* more confident, you will *feel* more confident.[15]

Finally, claim space. It's so easy to get stuck in your head when interviewing. But the interview doesn't happen in your head. It happens in the real world with a real person in a real place. *Arrive* in that space. Take it in. Allow your presence and your attention to engulf the entire building. This is how you show up. This is how you relate and connect with people.

When you step onto the property, take a moment to breathe and visually assess where you are. When you are waiting in the lobby, be aware of the entire room, the entire floor, the entire building. During your interview, let your presence fill the room and beyond.

Claiming space is especially important in panel and group interviews. When one person asks a question, answer to the whole group. When listening to a fellow interviewee, keep the interviewers in your awareness. You don't have to look or make eye contact to do this; simply be cognizant of the space.

It takes self-assurance to get out of your head and into the moment. Don't let your attention be focused only inwardly. Attend to the space around you to communicate confidence.

---

[15] Amy Cuddy. Presence: Bringing Your Boldest Self to Your Biggest Challenges. (London: Orion, 2016), 205.

The hiring manager has to be able to envision you in the position that you're interviewing for. So do you. Act as though you belong in the position. Demonstrate your comfort with the position and the company by breathing well, opening up, and claiming space, and you will communicate to the hiring manager that you have the confidence to handle the job.

— ◆ —

This should be obvious, but ... all of these things (especially breathing) *are* kinda obvious. But they all fly out the window when we're nervous. The point is to increase your awareness, especially under pressure. That takes practice.

16

Communicate Composedly

Silence is golden.

In the fall of 2010 during a gubernatorial debate, Arizona governor Jan Brewer made headlines for her now notorious "awkward pause." She lost her train of thought, held her breath and sat staring with her mouth open for several seconds. The video soon went viral on the Internet with comments such as "painful," "embarrassing" and "uncomfortable."

No wonder we're afraid to pause.

We think pausing will make people uncomfortable or we'll lose their attention. This is true, when the pause is poorly executed. However, skillful pausing adds meaning and intensity to what we're saying; without it we risk overwhelming our listeners. We want to appear calm, collected and composed in the interview, which is impossible without incorporating the pause.

The pause:

Assists our breathing. Pausing allows us to breathe. If we talk nonstop, it's impossible to breathe deeply. As mentioned, breathing well during an interview allows us to communicate confidently, remain calm and rational, and affects the interviewer as well.

Slows us down. For those of you who speak quickly when nervous (Show of hands? My hand's up!), the pause can assist you in slowing down. Speaking too quickly guarantees that you'll be viewed as erratic and hard to follow. Pausing often will slow down your speech, calm you down and make you appear more composed and confident.

Substitutes for space-fillers. Nothing loses credibility as quickly as peppering your speech with space-fillers such as "um," "uh" and "ok." Pausing after statements will force you to remove these common "space-wasters," increasing your professionalism.

Increases our intelligence. Well, perhaps it won't actually raise your IQ, but pausing will help you appear more intelligent. Often, when we're asked a question during an interview, we launch into our answers and lose our train of thought. **Pausing allows us time to think.** By pausing before answering, we can collect our thoughts and avoid verbal blunders. Breathing deeply during the pause assists us in getting more oxygen to the brain so we can think and speak intelligently.

Holds attention. Although we think the opposite is true, the pause holds attention if used correctly. Talking continuously encourages people to tune us out. "Incessant talker" is one of the top complaints of hiring managers. Nothing is more annoying than asking an interviewer a question and then being deluged with a never-ending monologue. Pausing acts as nonverbal punctuation. It frames our thoughts in an accessible way and helps us communicate more clearly. Use it judiciously to make your verbal presentation more powerful and memorable.

If you're afraid to pause because you think it will look or sound awkward, or you might lose the listener's attention, try this:

Use gestures. Some people gesture wildly, arms swinging back and forth while the listener ducks out of the way. Others look as though their arms are bound to their sides with invisible rope. To successfully incorporate the pause, you must learn how to gesture *effectively*. To maintain attention, gesture while speaking but **stop gesturing and freeze the hand in the air when pausing**. Freezing the hand gesture during the pause holds attention and makes your presentation stronger. Don't move until you begin speaking again.

This is harder than it sounds. Some people will freeze the hands momentarily when they pause, but then drop them. That doesn't count. Others will freeze the gesture but curl the fingers or pull the elbows to the waist during the pause. Still not right. My personal favorite has to be T-Rex gesturing: The person refuses to move their upper arms at all and gestures only from the elbows. Although dinosaurs are fun to watch in movies, they don't stand a chance in an interview.

Instead, to increase effectiveness, hold your hands perfectly still and outstretched during the pause, only moving them again once you begin speaking.

Breathe. The primary reason Governor Brewer's pause was deemed "awkward" was because she held her breath. If you watch the video you'll probably find that you hold your breath as well. Remember: Breathing patterns are contagious. When we pause and breathe we encourage others to breathe. In addition, we look intelligent and calm instead of nervous or awkward. Inhale deeply during the pause.

Close the lips. Close the lips after each statement. When Governor Brewer paused, it would have looked much less awkward had she closed her mouth. A gaping wide mouth looks silly. Closing the lips also serves as a kinesthetic reminder to pause instead of filling space with "ums" and "oks."

Limit verbal. In addition to incorporating the pause, also pay attention to *how much* you're talking. Less is more. Choose your words carefully and avoid adding extra verbiage when answering a question. Candidates who stay on-point, pause frequently and use gestures are seen as more intelligent, credible and confident.

Finally, if you lose your train of thought, look *down* while pausing. We tend to look up when trying to access a lost thought, but we end up looking like a boob.

Pause—just do it.

—◆—

This should be obvious, but ... pause means stop. As in, don't speak. Silence. Nada. You may think you're pausing but unless you create silence between phrases, it isn't a pause.

17

Communicate Appropriately

Honesty isn't always the best policy.

"Your name is Arabic, isn't it?" the hiring manager asked Anwar. Before Anwar could answer, the hiring manager asked, "Are you Muslim?" Unsure of how to answer, Anwar said yes. He felt the tone of the interview shift. He didn't get the job.

It is illegal to ask these types of questions, but that doesn't prevent hiring managers from doing so. Some hiring managers ask inappropriate questions because they know it's hard to prove discriminatory hiring practices, but most ask out of ignorance. In either case, savvy job seekers must communicate appropriately, regardless of the type of question asked. Prepare to answer illegal questions, so-called "trick" questions or just plain *weird* questions.

Illegal Questions.

It is tempting to stand up, righteously declare that the question just asked is illegal, and haughtily leave the interview, but I implore you to rethink this. Although questions asked by your interviewer may reveal that you don't want to work for this company, losing your temper will only backfire in the long run. People talk, and you won't be present to defend yourself and your actions when they do. Always act professionally, even when faced with illegal questions, rude interviewers or discriminatory hiring practices. You don't want to burn any bridges.

If you are asked an illegal question, you have two options. The first option is to turn the question around. Try, "May I ask how that pertains to the position?" or "I'm curious as to why you would ask that." Breathe deeply as you wait for your answer. Be sure to check in with your tone of voice; you <u>must</u> deliver the question calmly. Breathing will make all the difference here.

The second option is to unemotionally point out that the question is, in fact, illegal. To avoid sounding confrontational you must remain unattached— a tough challenge. While it is completely within your rights to calmly state a question is illegal, I rarely recommend this approach. Yet, should the hiring manager persist with unlawful questions, you may be forced to mention it.

Above all, keep your cool. Remember, most hiring managers ask illegal questions out of ignorance, and staying calm will go a long way in adding to your credibility.

Trick Questions.

Hiring managers sometimes ask trick questions in an attempt to get you to speak negatively. For example, "Have you ever been released from a job unfairly?" or "Tell me about a time your work was criticized." Sometimes even benign questions can fool you into speaking negatively, as in the following story:

"So why are you leaving your current job?" the hiring manager asked Adam.

"I just don't feel my talents are being used," he replied. "I tried to get my boss to see that I was willing to take on more responsibility, but he always gave the good projects to someone else even though I'm just as capable."

Although Adam tried to convey his drive and ambition, communicating negatively about his current job killed his interview immediately.

The words and phrases you choose speak more loudly than the words themselves. How you frame your comments and answers will translate nonverbally as either a positive or negative impression. Therefore, **frame everything positively.**

For example, Adam could have responded, "I'm looking for a position with more responsibility. I've learned a lot at my current job, and I am looking forward to improving my skills and challenging myself with new opportunities."

Weird Questions.

- *"If you were a candy bar, what kind would you be?"*
- *"How many gas stations are there in the United States?"*
- *"Why are manhole covers round?"*

The number one thing to keep in mind when answering "weird" questions is that hiring managers don't care so much about the content of your answer, but *how* you answer. Hiring managers ask these questions to see how you process information. They will watch how you react to the shock of being asked such a weird question, and how you come up with an answer.

First, pause and look down to communicate that you're considering the question thoughtfully. Take a deep breath so you don't get flustered or thrown off. Then look up and give the first answer that comes to mind. If you're breathing well, it doesn't matter what you say, just that you state it calmly and confidently.

I'm not advocating dishonesty. But there is a big difference between deceitfulness and caution. Refuse to answer illegal questions and frame the questions you do answer in a positive light. Although you might want to share that your current boss is a nutcase or that the hours are awful, don't. Speaking negatively, losing your temper or getting flustered will cost you the job, and possibly taint your reputation in the industry.

—◆—

This should be obvious, but ... always keep your cool, in every circumstance. One candidate blew his top because the interview started late. Do you think he got the job?

18

Communicate Sensitively

What's in it for me?

The interview had gone well. Jared felt rapport with the hiring manager, had answered questions with ease and believed he was a shoo-in.

But then the hiring manager asked, "Do you have any questions?"

And that's when Jared blew it. "My last job required a lot of weekend hours," he said. "Will I be required to work weekends?"

Suddenly the hiring manager's demeanor changed. He answered the question, but something shifted. Jared left, confused, and was even more disappointed when he received a rejection letter a week later.

Jared neglected to communicate sensitively.

"What types of medical benefits does this job provide?"

"How much vacation time do I get?"

"What's your sick time policy?"

Ask even one of the above questions and you risk losing the position. Why? Hiring managers listen for the hidden meaning behind your questions. To a hiring manager, asking about medical benefits says, "I have health problems." Asking about vacation says, "I care more about time off than working." Asking about sick time says, "I plan on calling in sick."

Whether you *mean* to communicate these things or not is beside the point. Your questions convey an agenda—real or imagined—to the hiring manager. If you neglect to communicate sensitively, you may be screened out due to the underlying messages you send through your questions.

But isn't the interview a chance to get questions answered? In a word, no. Never forget that in the mind of the hiring manager, you are a risk until proven otherwise. Anything you say in an interview can be used against you in the hiring process.

Many job seekers ask these questions upfront to save time. In fact, many interview preparation books suggest you do this to identify whether or not you want to work for the company. Bad advice. Asking what's-in-it-for-me type questions in an interview won't save you time—unless you plan on standing up and leaving the interview upon hearing an unsatisfactory answer. And if you receive positive answers to your questions? Great! You'll know this is a company you want to work for. But upon hearing your questions, the hiring manager may decide *he* no longer wants to work with *you*.

The time to get your questions answered is after you've been offered the position, *in writing*. Keep in mind that everything—pay, vacation, benefits, etc.—is negotiable.

For example, when my husband, Kevin, interviewed for his promotion, he was pretty sure he wouldn't accept the position unless offered a specific pay increase. Yet he was careful not to mention this in the interview. He knew that asking for more than management wanted to offer would take him out of the running immediately. He wanted to hear the offer before making a final decision. He also viewed the interview as an opportunity to talk up his strengths to management and float his ideas for improving the kitchen, regardless of whether they ultimately offered him the job. Most importantly, he recognized that if offered the promotion, he would be in a stronger position to negotiate salary. Management would be more willing to discuss compensation once they'd invested time in choosing a final candidate.

In the end, that's exactly what happened. They offered Kevin the position and stated the pay increase, which was less than Kevin wanted. He agreed to accept the position at the stated rate with the stipulation that they guarantee an even bigger pay increase in 90 days. They agreed.

I'm not suggesting you avoid asking questions at all. You'll want to ask questions in the interview to find out more about the company and to communicate your enthusiasm for the position. But communicate sensitively by asking *appropriate* questions.

What constitutes an "appropriate question?"

Ask the hiring manager to tell you more about the position. As mentioned previously, asking your interviewer to talk about the position will give you valuable insight about what the company is really looking for and help you interview more effectively.

Ask about the person who previously occupied the position. Ask what this person did that was particularly helpful as well as what they might have done differently to get inside information you can use to highlight your relevant skills and experience.

Ask about expectations. Ask what type of progress the hiring manager expects from the person who ultimately wins the position.

One last caution: The hiring manager may ask *you* questions (about benefits and pay, for example) hoping you'll betray your true priorities. Don't be fooled. Reply that you don't have questions at this time but that you look forward to learning more.

The interview is neither the time nor place to get your questions answered. Wait until an offer has been extended. Once you possess a written offer, feel free to ask questions and negotiate.

—◆—

This should be obvious, but ... don't ask what the sexual harassment policy is, or how casual "casual Friday" is or how late you can be to work without being considered "late." Really.

19

Communicate Patiently

Never call to follow-up.

PUT DOWN THE PHONE AND BACK AWAY SLOWLY. I know you're anxious. And I understand you want to make sure they don't forget you. But hear this: **There is absolutely nothing you can do to change the impression you made at the interview**. <u>Nothing</u>. Well, except calling to follow-up. That can turn your good impression into a bad one.

If you've followed the advice in this book, you <u>will</u> interview successfully. So please, don't call and screw it up.

Cynthia Shapiro, in her book, *What Does Somebody Need to Do to Get a Job Around Here? 44 Insider Secrets and Tips That Will Get You Hired* shares a story that illustrates this point.[16] A hiring manager, after conducting interviews for several

---

[16] Shapiro 136.

months, decided on his first choice. As he began background checks and calling references, the candidate called to clarify something he said in the interview. The hiring manager found that a bit odd, but assured him that everything was fine. A few days later, the candidate called to check on his status. The hiring manager told him that he was one of the top candidates, things were proceeding normally and he had nothing to worry about. Imagine the hiring manager's surprise when he learned that the candidate had called not one, but two additional times. At this point, the hiring manager wondered how confident this candidate really was, and how this neediness would play out on the job. He made an offer to his second choice.

We think that repetition makes us stand out in the eyes of the hiring manager; but calling to follow-up makes you appear desperate and needy. As we've seen, nonverbal communication is more than what you do with your eyes, body and voice. It includes your resume, the objects you bring with you, clothing, and in this case, *what you leave unsaid.* By refusing to make the follow-up call you nonverbally communicate your confidence.

Do send a short note thanking the interviewer for his or her time and reiterating your enthusiasm for the position. But then leave it. Really. Don't call.

Hiring managers don't need to be reminded of who you are. (Numerous job seekers believe that hiring managers all suffer from bad memories…) If you've properly communicated in the interview, there's nothing left for you to do but wait. I've never heard of a situation where a hiring manager was on the fence about a candidate, received a follow-up call, and based on the phone call, offered the candidate the job. In fact, there is a greater chance that in calling to follow-up you will hurt your chances. Be patient. Breathe. Stay calm.

Let your interview stand on its own.

—◆—

This should be obvious, but … if the hiring manager invites you to call to check status, then of course, do it.

76

20

Communicate Optimistically

If you don't get the job, don't get discouraged.

The letter arrives, you open it and read: "Company XYZ would like to thank you for your time. We regret to inform you that we've chosen another candidate…"

No doubt about it, it's discouraging to find out you didn't get the job. What you do with that discouragement, however, can decide the outcome of your next interview.

As mentioned, companies want to hire positive and enthusiastic candidates. These emotions can't be "put on." Regardless of your disappointment, you must approach each interview with a renewed sense of optimism.

Dejected, negative and angry candidates don't stand a chance. Stay positive and approach each interview as if it were your first.

Here are a few tips to help you keep your chin up:

Debrief each interview carefully. After the interview you may get in the car and begin mentally berating yourself for "mistakes." Be careful. When you debrief, do it in *third* person. Although it feels funny at first, using third person language will help you objectively assess your interview. Instead of using "I" statements—"I shouldn't have mentioned that" or "I was speaking too fast"—review your interview as though you were watching and coaching someone else—"David shouldn't have mentioned that" or "David was speaking too fast."

Now, tell yourself what you'll do better next time in *first* person: "I'll take my time before answering and focus on breathing deeply. I'll pause more often, and use more gesturing."

Remind yourself that each interview is an opportunity. Every time you interview you refine your skills. Although we hope every interview we attend will be our last (my apologies to the weirdos out there who love interviewing), if we don't get the job, we must remind ourselves the opportunity wasn't wasted. The only way to get better at interviewing is to interview. Practice makes perfect!

No may not mean no. Typically, we receive the rejection letter and think the door has closed permanently for that particular position. But this isn't always the case. Many times the hiring manager's first choice doesn't work out; if you've interviewed well, the hiring manager may ask you to consider taking the position. This actually happened at FORTE. After our first candidate didn't work out, I called and offered the position to our second choice. Unfortunately, she had already taken another job. I then reached out to our third choice who ended up taking the job and is still with us today. View every interview as a chance to expand your network. Be gracious. Thank the interviewer for his or her time. Stay in contact. You never know what may happen down the road.

Approach each subsequent interview with a fresh outlook. No matter how many interviews you've performed, approach every interview with an optimistic attitude. Thinking thoughts like, "What's the difference? I probably

78

won't get this job either," will translate! Our thoughts are more powerful than we imagine.

Replenish yourself. Looking for work is mentally, emotionally and physically exhausting. You must take time to replenish yourself or you'll end up depleted. Take time for exercise. Eat well and drink lots of water. Get enough sleep. Read a book to unwind before going to bed or take a bath. Make sure to schedule time with friends and family. This will assist you in presenting your very best when in an interview.

The job you've been waiting for is right around the corner. I believe it, and so should you. Keep this hope in the forefront of your mind and it <u>will</u> come across in the interview.

—◆—

This should be obvious, but ... you're not alone! Check your area for local resources like job seekers' groups. It can be beneficial to meet with others who are looking for work. Who knows, you might find a connection that leads to your dream job!

21

Communicate Authentically

Be yourself.

Persuasively… calmly… intelligently… carefully… Yes, you need to communicate all these ways in order to demonstrate you are the right person for the job. Yet above all, if I had to choose one communication "tip" over the others, I'd say:

Be yourself.

The most important thing you can communicate in an interview is who you are. You can't trick people into believing you're something you're not, nor is that the intention of this book. We want to present ourselves in the best light possible, not "put on a show."

Because we are often unaware of what we communicate nonverbally, we inadvertently get in our own way. We mean to say one thing and end up expressing something entirely different. How many times have you said, or heard someone else say, "But that's not what I *meant*!" Nonverbal communication transmits the majority of the message. Increasing our nonverbal intelligence helps us communicate clearly; when we understand and are aware of nonverbal communication, we ensure that our intended message gets across.

By tuning into your nonverbal communication you'll be able to convey your qualifications and your enthusiasm. You'll be able to speak calmly and confidently, but also show that you're listening. You'll be able to remain composed and patient, and yet purposefully avoid behaviors, apparel and objects that detract from your presentation. In other words, you'll be able to be *you*, without all the other stuff getting in the way.

So my parting advice to you is this: Take a breath, believe in yourself and use the skills in this book to allow the real you to shine in the interview. The most powerful way to communicate in an interview, and in life, is authentically.

Epilogue

Hired! Now what?

Congratulations! You've been awarded the position. It feels terrific to hear a hiring manager say, "We'd like to offer you the job."

Increasing your nonverbal intelligence helped secure your new position, but you can't afford to ignore it going forward. Getting along with colleagues, delivering negative information, giving presentations—all of these common workplace scenarios require that you communicate well. Communicating at work is no different than in an interview—you'll still need to pay attention to your content, delivery and reception.

With that in mind, I'll leave you with my Top Five Nonverbal Tips for the Workplace:

Tip #1: *Increase your awareness.*

Continue to increase your nonverbal intelligence by increasing your awareness. Watch how your voice pattern affects those around you or how changing your posture affects the way people respond. You can observe this during presentations, meetings or just stopping to talk to a colleague in the hall. **Effective communicators pay attention to the nonverbal messages they send and receive.**

Tip #2: *Expand your skills.*

When it comes to communication, we fall back on what's "comfortable." But what's comfortable isn't always effective. Having only one way of communicating limits us. Nonverbally intelligent people communicate a variety of ways. Get coaching, sign up for a workshop or do additional reading on non-verbal skills. Remember, **nonverbal communication translates the majority of any message.**

Tip #3: *Adapt to the situation.*

Once you increase your awareness, you can adapt your approach. Perhaps you'll stand with your weight evenly distributed when conducting a meeting, but lean forward and nod your head when listening. **Nonverbally intelligent people vary their approach as needed.** Adjusting your style to suit the circumstance allows for smooth communication.

Tip #4: *Monitor your breathing.*

When you begin using your new communication skills, consider your breathing. As previously stated, shallow breathing affects the sound of your voice, your gesturing, and most importantly, your confidence. Low, abdominal breathing leads to rational thinking by providing more oxygen to the brain—crucial for dealing with conflict. Breathing well can affect the emotional state of those around us, as well as our own. **Excellent communicators monitor their breathing at all times.**

Tip #5: *Redefine success.*

Successful communicators understand that they cannot choose their reality; they can only choose their response to reality. Therefore, **nonverbal intelligence is about controlling ourselves, not about reading and controlling other people.** By understanding the nonverbal components of communication, we increase our options. We can observe an interaction and adapt our approach because we know what to look for, not because we hope to control or dominate. When we let go of controlling the outcome, we truly become successful.

Let me say once again, congratulations! I wish you the best in all your endeavors.

Case Study #1

Ever wonder what interview coaching looks like? How we work with clients, the FORTE way, on interview skills? Maybe you're wondering if it really works? Here are the stories of two coaching clients.*

John, coached by Sari:

John* came in for a coaching session at the behest of his wife, who was, ironically, a career coach. He had run a construction business for ten years until the economy tanked in 2009, forcing him to close his company. He had done contract work off and on ever since, but had now been unemployed for over a year, and really wanted a job where he could invest his time and talents.

John was feeling pretty dejected when he came in; he'd never been unemployed in his life. He had a software development background, a degree in computer science and held an MBA. Before he started his construction company he had always been recruited from one job to the next.

John had been on several interviews before he came to see me, but they never seemed to turn into a job offer. He was tired of going from interview to interview and getting the dreaded rejection letter. What was he doing wrong?

I started, as we usually do here at FORTE, with some mock interview questions and immediately sensed that something was "off." Where before John answered my questions with a big booming voice and a hearty laugh, once we started role-playing he seemed…small. He sat with his shoulders tucked in, hands in his lap and was overly polite.

I stopped the role-play and asked John what he considered his interviewing weakness to be. He answered, "I think I have a tendency to come on too strong. I have a big personality and I think that scares people." His answer shocked me because none of that "big personality" was coming through!

I said, "Here's what I think is happening. You do have a big personality, and perhaps you did come on too strong in previous interviews, but now you've gone the opposite direction. This is a mistake. A hiring manager's number one fear is that they hire the wrong person. It's your job to communicate that you are the person they've been looking for all along. So let's look at how to do that without coming on 'too strong.'"

I started by having John take in the space around him. "You are only focusing on the space between you and the interviewer, which is making you appear small and unsure of yourself. If you really want to command the room without being arrogant, you need to communicate with an awareness of the entire room." I had John look around the room and take deep breaths. I then asked him another mock question and as he spoke told him to keep the entire room in his awareness. Suddenly his voice sounded more confident. He seemed bigger. He sat up taller.

I then asked him to sit up straight instead of leaning back and to gesture as he talked. This made him appear more credible and engaged. I said, "If someone were to watch you without any sound, they would assume you were the person in charge!"

Finally I told him to watch how he spoke. When he first answered my questions he said things like, "I think," "I believe" and "in my opinion." I told him to get rid of these "softeners" and instead speak like an expert. Use language like, "Here's the problem. Your competitors are ahead of the game because…" Or "Here's how I would handle this…" He needed to talk like the expert he was and communicate he was an excellent fit. He also needed to stop being so timid and instead breathe deeply and communicate with confidence.

At that point our hour was over. John left and promised to let me know how the interview went. A few days later he let me know he nailed the interview, and a week after that I learned he was offered the job.

Case Study #2

Lisa, coached by Rachel:

Lisa* had just graduated with a nursing degree when she came for a coaching session with me. "I'm getting discouraged," she said. "I love nursing and I'm excited to get my career going, but I'm having a hard time in the interviews. I'm starting to wonder if I'll ever get a job." She was bright, cheerful, and sharp as a tack. So what was the problem?

We role played a few interview questions and I could soon see that Lisa's eagerness to be liked overshadowed her ability to communicate competence. "A nurse is so much more than a caring person," I told her. "Yes, we want to know that nurses are real people who care about their patients, but in order to be hired in that field you have to demonstrate that you're a hard-worker who can work well under pressure, attend to important details, and prioritize in a crisis. You have to communicate that you care *and* that you're competent."

Lisa's natural voice pattern and body language were almost exclusively Approachable. She smiled and nodded perpetually, leaving no doubt that she was enthusiastic about nursing and really cared about people. The only time she allowed her voice to curl down at the ends of statements in an Authoritative voice pattern was when she was giving what she thought was the "right" answer to a question. But then she lost her personality. "Oh no," I said, laughing. "Now you sound like an encyclopedia!" Through her coaching session we worked on pairing her enthusiasm with the Authoritative voice pattern so that both her personality and credibility could shine through.

In addition, Lisa was, understandably, nervous. "I'm even more nervous now," she told me, "after having a few interviews and not getting the job." But that nervousness was showing up as anxiety—her shallow breathing made her voice sound edgy and damaged her credibility. She didn't feel confident, and it showed.

We practiced some deep breathing exercises and some power poses. "It's normal," I told her, "to feel nervous at an interview. You don't want to be so relaxed they think you don't care! But you do want to demonstrate that you can be calm and confident in times of stress. A nurse HAS to be able to think even when everything is going nuts around her. You demonstrate your ability to do that by handling the interview with composure."

She had great answers for the interview questions I threw out at her once she was able to breathe! "Take a breath once you hear the question," I reminded her. "Just pause and breathe and the answer will come to you. You know your stuff! Remember, you are composing *yourself* during the pause, not composing your answer. The answer is already there."

Lisa's coaching session could not have been more perfectly timed. She had two interviews with two different hospitals in the following week. And guess what – she got job offers from both of them! She was able to pick the situation that best suited her lifestyle. Later, she sent me a thank you note for the coaching session. She wrote, "I got my dream job because of it!"

*You didn't think we'd actually use their real names, did you? We do work with rock stars, but ones who appreciate that we're not name dropping all the time.

About the Author

Sari de la Motte, who has been described as a "guru of the unspoken," is the CEO and founder of FORTE. She is a sought-after keynote speaker and trial consultant, providing keynotes for conferences, workshops for organizations, in-house training and coaching for corporations and consulting for high-profile jury trials. Sari holds a Bachelor of Music Education and Master of Science in Teaching, and has taught on the faculty of Pacific University and Portland State University.

Sari engages her audience by sharing the power of nonverbal communication with relevant examples, practical applications and humor. She is not a "body language expert." Instead of focusing on reading the body language of others, her work concentrates on how we can communicate more clearly by working on our *own* communication.

Sari blogs regularly about workplace issues at her blog "Jam Session" (www.nonverbalFORTE.com/blog), and has been featured in The Oregonian, Willamette Week, The Atlantic, and the Huffington Post. For more interview resources visit www.nonverbalFORTE.com/interviewtips.

Sari is passionately committed to sharing the power of nonverbal communication with others, and believes effective communication is the key to increased influence in the educational, corporate, and personal realm.

Sari is based in Portland, Oregon. To learn more about Sari or FORTE, visit: www.nonverbalFORTE.com

Bibliography

Cuddy, Amy. *Presence: Bringing Your Boldest Self to Your Biggest Challenges.* London: Orion, 2016.

Darlington, Joy and Nancy Schuman. *The Everything Job Interview Book: All You Need to Make a Great First Impression and Land the Perfect Job.* Avon, Mass: Adams Media. 2008.

Davis, Brian. *Top Notch Interviews. Tips, Tricks, and Techniques from the First Call to Getting the Job You Want.* Franklin Lakes, NJ: Career Press. 2010.

Gladwell, Malcolm. *Blink: The Power of Thinking Without Thinking.* New York: Back Bay Books. 2007.

Grinder, Michael. *Managing Groups: The Inside Track.* Stout Graphics. 2008

Krannich, Ronald L., and Caryl Krannich. *You Should Hire Me! Interview Secrets to Get the Job You Love.* Manassas Park, VA: Impact Publications. 2008.

Peper, E. and V. Tibbetts. "Effects of Paced Breathing on Inhalation Volumes," *Proceedings of the Twenty-first Annual Meeting of the Association for Applied Psychophysiology and Biofeedback.* Wheat Ridge, CO: Apb. 1990.

Shapiro, Cynthia. *What Does Somebody Have to Do to Get a Job Around Here? 44 Insider Secrets That Will Get You Hired.* New York: St. Martin's Griffin. 2008

Vega, Lizandra. *The Image of Success: Make a Great Impression and Land the Job You Want.* New York: American Management Association. 2010.

www.ingramcontent.com/pod-product-compliance
Lightning Source LLC
Chambersburg PA
CBHW060632210326
41520CB00010B/1572